1 2 3

Carol Watson
Illustrated by David Higham

Consultant: Wyn Brooks
Deputy-Head Teacher of the Coombes School,
Arborfield, Berkshire; lectures widely on
Primary School Mathemetics.

This is Bella the elephant.

She lives in the zoo.

2

one

Bella has one tail and one trunk.

3

There are two camels in the zoo.

Each camel has two humps.

two

Can you count them?

How many giraffes can you see?

The giraffes have spots on their necks.

three

Which giraffe has three spots on its neck?

The polar bears love playing by their pool

How many bears are there?

8

How many legs does each
polar bear have?

four

Five zebras live in the zoo.

Which zebra has five stripes?

five

Six crocodiles are playing by the water.

6

Can you see their sharp teeth?

12

One of the crocodiles has six teeth?

six

Which one is it?

Seven kangaroos like jumping up and down.

Each kangaroo has a baby in its pouch.

seven

How many babies are there?

There are eight leopards in the zoo.

They like watching the birds.

eight

How many birds are there?

There are nine penguins in the zoo?

9

They like eating fish.

18

How many fish are there?

nine

Ten monkeys are playing in a tree.

10

Can you see which tail belongs
to each monkey?

ten

How many tails can you find?

The zoo keeper has lost some of his animals.

Can you find one polar bear, two crocodiles, three leopards and four monkeys?

How many animals are missing?

Can you count the zoo animals?

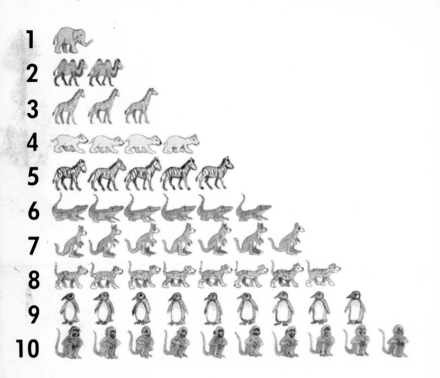

1
2
3
4
5
6
7
8
9
10

First published in 1984
Usborne Publishing Ltd
20 Garrick St, London
WC2E 9BJ, England
© Usborne Publishing Ltd 1984

The name of Usborne and the
device 🦇 are Trade Marks of
Usborne Publishing Ltd.

Printed in Portugal